KU-175-064

wild embers

wild embers

poems of rebellion, fire and beauty

NIKITA GILL

First published in Great Britain in 2017 by Trapeze
an imprint of The Orion Publishing Group Ltd
Carmelite House, 50 Victoria Embankment
London EC4Y 0DZ

An Hachette UK Company

5 7 9 10 8 6

Copyright © Nikita Gill 2017

The moral right of Nikita Gill to be identified as
the author of this work has been asserted in accordance
with the Copyright, Designs and Patents Act of 1988.

All rights reserved. No part of this publication may be
reproduced, stored in a retrieval system, or transmitted
in any form or by any means, electronic, mechanical,
photocopying, recording, or otherwise, without the
prior permission of both the copyright owner and the
above publisher of this book.

A CIP catalogue record for this book is
available from the British Library.

ISBN 978 1 4091 7392 2
ISBN (eBook) 978 1 4091 7393 9

Printed and bound by CPI Group (UK) Ltd, Croydon, CR0 4YY

www.orionbooks.co.uk

For you
and all the fires
you will
give birth to.

Contents

Someone I loved once told me that there are fragments within us that are the same age as the universe, and because we are matter, we can never be destroyed. That a part of us will live forever and ever, and that in making us the universe was celebrating itself, we are its living, breathing joy.

Miracle

It took 3.8 billion years
of triumphant evolution,
remarkable collision,
an unbelievable confluence
made by sheer will and influence
of this infinite universe
and all of the stars
to get you here.

I hope you never doubt again
that even when you are in pain,
that you are a miracle,
that every part of you is incredible.

Multiverse

The growing, aching quiet of this home
has led me to reading space theories.
The notions are slowly wrapping around my bones,
settling between my heart and ribcage with intricacy.

When I feel most bereft in this aching grief,
I find soothing in the words of a philosopher.
William James explained the multiverse in brief,
but with the foresight of an astronomer.

He spoke of time as a non-linear vision,
that the universe is not one but many,
a different one spun off every one of our decisions,
therefore the versions of us that exist are plenty.

How comforting to think
that there are so many universes.
Perhaps one where the Titanic did not sink,
one where humanity is kind to the earth, not a curse.

Possibly one where magic is real
where faith is rewarded instead of scorned.
And perhaps even one where I do not grieve,
because you are alive and I have no need to mourn.

The Meaning of a Day

Each new dawn brings with it
15 new reasons for laughs,
100,000 new heartbeats in your chest,
your lifeblood voyages 168,000,000 miles.

And each new morning on this earth translates
7,200 earthquakes in the upcoming 24 hours.
More than 18,000 thunderstorms,
our planet is struck by lightning 8.6 million times.

And in space?
The passing of a day
means the wondrous birth of
approximately 275 billion stars.

This is why everyday
is an opportunity for rebirth.
That is why no matter what they say,
you must never underestimate your own worth.

The Possibility in Impossibility

Yesterday, you spoke to me
about impossibilities
and how certain relationships
lives and moments were not destined to be.

For you, I collected these;
in hope that if you do not trust me,
at least you will believe
these facts from the galaxies.

On Venus (and yes, I know, you will find this bizarre),
it snows in metal and rains in sulphuric acid
and a teaspoon of a dancing neutron star
weighs more than everyone together in the world.

What I am trying to say, my darling,
is that I know you said you wouldn't survive this day
but across our beautiful universe,
what is impossible is happening everyday.

Growth

Maybe the true meaning of life
is to understand that
you have never been
in the same physical place twice,
not even within your own home.

You see, the earth,
the solar system
and the galaxy are all moving
through space
constantly.

And from this,
you learn that growth
is an essential part
of flowing,
of being.

That growth is simply
learning how to suffer,
gracefully, elegantly
constantly moving and travelling
without letting your pain tear you apart.

And take solace in the fact
that even though growth itself is agonising
your spirit was never meant
to feel the same pain,
the same grief twice.

Dark Matter

There is grace in the way
the sinews of your ribcage
contain this heart of yours.
This magic thing in your chest
that defies science
in how many times it breaks
and brings itself back to life again.

And every time you thought it dead
love flowed through it like electricity
starting up what you thought was dead.
You spend so much time wondering,
'What gives this thing
I thought dead
the energy to start again?'

The answer lies in that 80 per cent
of your heart you have not yet channeled.
There are stars glittering inside you
that have never been handled.
This, the dark matter of you
hides an immeasurable amount of strength
and an impossible amount of energy.

It lies dormant,
solid and silent, like the 80 per cent
of space yet unexplored.
This means that when you believe you are empty
that the world has drained you completely,
there is still an impossible amount of your strength
simply awaiting discovery.

The dark matter of you,
a powerhouse of impossibility.
Which goes to show you
the resilient human heart is a thing
of intergalactic,
interwoven,
incredible rarity.

Venus

Decide tonight,
to take a lesson from Venus,
she shines brighter than any planet.

A morning
and evening star,
in our endless sky.

She hasn't a single moon
to worship her
or to cloud her judgement.

She is alone.
And oh
how brilliantly she shines.

The Sun and the Moon

Aim for a love
that reminds you
of the devotion
the sun has to the moon.

Whether she is in fractions
or she is whole,
he still shrouds his intense light
in the darkness of the night.

To give her the entire sky,
without judgement,
so she can shine in any way
she wants to.

You deserve someone
who adores you
on the days you are
in broken fragments too.

You deserve someone
who lets you glow
in every way
you need to.

Dark Days

On the darkest days,
I look at the stars,
and marvel at
the patchwork of time
staring back at me.

Not a single burst of starlight is the same age,
some of these stars
are born billions of years apart,
yet travel through time together
making this beautiful piece of art.

Sometime, somewhere,
these stars have already encountered
a better version of me
on her best day looking up at them
and thanking them for helping me see.

Your Heart is not a Hospital

Your body is not a first aid kit
for broken people
and damaged souls
and hearts that are too tired
to fix themselves.

Your heart is not a hospital
to rejuvenate
and spend all of its life blood
on other people's problems
and sadnesses.

You have been created
from the blood
of incalculable planets
and immense supernovas
and infinite constellations.

And they didn't spend years
painting your soul
into masterpiece-like existence
for you to waste it on someone
who doesn't appreciate you.

A Conversation with My Mental Illness

Every sleepless night I am interrogated
by the darkness that lives inside of me.

It says to me:
'You are pointless.'

I respond:
'No one in this world is pointless.'

It scowls at me:
'You are a terrible person.'

I admit:
'I am a good person who did terrible things.'

It rages at me:
'No one needs you.'

I counter:
'There are people who have adored me.'

It seethes at me:
'And what of those who hated you?'

I sigh:
'Being unforgiving of others is a sign of insecurity.'

It finally explodes:
'I will make sure you always doubt yourself!'

And every night
I gather my courage
as my armour and say:
'And whenever you do,
I will look at the vastness
of the ever changing sky
the presence of a moon
that helps the sea
the same sunset that has been going
around the earth
for billions of years
and remind myself
that the same universe that made them
and gave them such *purpose*
also made me.
And nothing you say to me
will ever convince me otherwise
because that is a fact
I will never question about my journey.'

Unlearning

Womanhood
is rich with unlearning.
How to unlearn the way
you hate your body,
how to rebuild your spirit
after the supernova of love
finally bursts,
how to understand that
there are a million
new versions of you,
hiding under your skin.
How each one is born
from suffering agonisingly,
unlearning what others
want you and your body to be,
finding moments
and seconds by metaphors
in everything
that makes you feel good
make you feel
how you are supposed
to feel.
Reiterating them
till there is finally understanding
and accepting,

inside your very soul
the only thing that truly matters
is how often you say
on your journey,
'This, all of this,
is for me.'

Black Hole

In space,
a black hole
is an expanse of cosmos
having a pull so great
that nothing,
no matter
can escape.

In human beings,
a black hole
is spending your energy
loving someone
who takes all of your love
and gives back nothing
in return.

Ghost Story

Ask me my favourite ghost story
and I will tell you the one
about your haunted house heart
still housing all the people you used to be.

The child inside you
you thought life had taken
the person who was full of joy
that tragedy had broken.

You imagined they had left you
that those parts of you
that made you incandescent
and valuable are gone.

What no one ever told you
was that nothing ever really dies
not if it matters to you
your memories keep it alive.

It is the law of the universe
that even ghosts understand
as long as they matter to someone
they still exist and in your heart they stand.

Ghosts of the person you used to be
are so proud of who you are,
they live on inside you applauding you
for living on despite your scars.

Lonely

Who has been lying in your world?
Who has been betraying
your innocent and yet pure soul
by telling you that this should be easy?
Who has been saying
that people are not temporary?

Tell me, do you truly believe
the big bang wasn't agony?
That our planet's birth was not made
by coming out of misery?
That our solar system's creation
in the universe's womb was easy?

The loneliest thing
you can ever do
is take every instance
where you should grow
and waste it by only thinking
how could this happen to you?

Endings

Look at the way
the stars burn
in the night sky.

Look at the entrails
they leave as they are
passing us by.

They are dying,
and death
is meant to be ugly.

Painful and destructive,
it is made
through tragedy.

And yet
when a star dies
it is still lovely.

Which is to say,
not everything
dies violently.

Sometimes
it is the way things end
that is beautiful.

Even when things
are raw and aching
the endings are still magical.

The greatest magic you have is the
courage you go digging for,
when your world falls apart,
the light you still hold,
when everything has grown dark.

Witch

We are the blood
of the witches
you thought were dead.

We carry witchcraft in our bones
whilst the magic still sings
inside our heads.

When the witch hunters
imprisoned our ancestors
when they tried to burn the magic away.

Someone should have
warned them
that magic cannot be tamed.

Because you cannot burn away
what has always
been aflame.

Magic

The greatest wish
I have ever had
is to create with words,
what wizards cannot
and what magic
never has.

The most elegant bond
I can ever pray for
is aiding in the recovery
of someone who is made of wreckage
and facilitating their becoming
their own hero in their story.

Dragon's Breath

Girls like you
were born
to tame dragons,
to fight in wars,
to lead armies.

Girls like you
were created
to swallow darkness,
to quell monsters,
to destroy obscurity.

Girls like you
were given life,
to bring tempests
and hail gales,
unto their enemies.

Don't let a king
or a prince
or a fairytale
tell you you are smaller than that
or who you are meant to be.

Sorcery

Everyday, I magic myself alive again
from the near death experience of trauma.

I swallow my heart back from
the lump it has become in my throat.

I taste my own memories
without the flavour of blood but as poetry.

I learn how to whisper my name
without it sounding like a curse.

I murmur spells to the parts of me
others have found too dangerous to love.

And after this morning ritual
I finally smile at the woman in my mirror.

Tell me again,
how healing is not a magical thing.

Tell me again,
how I am not made of sorcery.

With Love From Midnight

When the day's mistakes
are too much to bear,
when everything feels
like devastation beyond repair,
remind yourself:
how mystical it is that everyday,
the clocks reset to 00.00
the reason they say
midnight is the witching hour,
is because a new day rises
from the ashes of the old,
embers breathe new life to its fire,
giving us a chance to mend,
a chance to restore
all that is broken
and what you thought was lost.

The Art of Unmissing

I have been incanting my heart
in how to unmiss you,
spelling myself into mastering the art
of forgetting the damage
you have done stitching back my soul
from the savage way you ripped it apart.
I think I finally know
where I went wrong.

You see, yesterday, someone asked me,
'How do you heal
from losing
the greatest love of your life?'

I smiled and answered,
'You make yourself another one.
And you make
that love yourself.'

Wolves

The thing I admire most
about you
is no matter how hard,
or how much the world
has tried to
beat you,
break you,
destroy you,
and throw you to the wolves
you are still here,
turning all your pain
all your suffering
into armour,
into determination,
into weapons
and earning the respect
of that same pack of wolves
that were meant to rip you
limb from limb.

Your Trauma

Your trauma has a name.
It sleeps besides you at night.
It reminds you every morning of your shame.
It watches you swallow your pride.

It snarls at you from the grocery aisle,
it sneers at you when you drive,
it follows you from place to place,
making you wish you weren't alive.

It hides in the living room,
it buries holes in your heart,
it makes you feel hopeless,
you are so close to falling apart.

This terrible thing, this broken thing,
tells you you belong to it,
this miserable thing, this despicable thing,
tells you that you can't survive without it.

But what your trauma doesn't realise,
and what your trauma doesn't see,
is how by simply surviving it
it is daring you to beat it, to *be*.

When Love Dies

There is no magic in the way love dies.
It closes away into something tragic,
and no matter how much poets
and singers romanticise it,
try to turn it into
something great and beautiful,
something artistic and incredible,
painted with the silver
of a thousand sweet moons
and the gold of millions
of sparkling sun's rays,
I will always compare love's death
to the way a hunted wild thing dies.
Alone, betrayed
and desperately fighting
against all odds
to stay alive.

Burning

A woman is most powerful when she leaves
the man who broke her body into purple pieces,
but is now trying to drown her in his apologies,
that then dissolve into a sea of acidic threats.

He will burn her,
he promises
He will shred her skin
to make into kindling.

But this time,
she does not fear it,
this time,
she faces him and says:

'There is burning
And there is you
and I would rather choose burning
than ever return to you.'

Why I am Magic

There are days
I have been the thirst
and days
when I have been the water
but the days
I love myself most
are the days I am both.

The Well Spoken Heart

The less you listen
to the whispered words
of your gentle heart,
the more you choose to ignore it,
the more you build
the kind of wall around it
that no one
can climb to get to hold it.

Instead,
listen to what it wants
and let it tell you what it needs
and you will find
it growing roots
and thriving
when you plant
these mystical seeds.

Conjuring

There is a conjuring
within us all
a whisper in the air
a call to arms
like an incantation
or the beginning
of the kind of storm
that brings about
change,
transformation.

Some call it
sisterhood,
Some call it
Feminism
But another word
for this paradigm shift
is simply called
revolution.

Wolf and Woman

Some days,
I am both wolf and woman
and I am still learning
how to apologise
for my wild.

Anger

The anger
is like a demon
trying to escape into your spirit,
it claws at your insides
a darkness that relishes
the pain it will cause.

If you keep it
in the pit of your stomach
if you hold it inside your ribcage too long
it will take your tongue prisoner
when you least suspect it
and terrorise everyone you love.

This fiend,
this cruel thing
it can be defeated,
it does not own you
it deserves no space
inside your spirit.
Instead,
channel it,
find a way to let it out
cry, dance, sing, build, create,
do everything you can
to give it a way out.

Take everything that
tries to destroy you
curse you,
and turn it
into something beautiful
by incantation.

Learned Helplessness

They call it 'learned helplessness'
finally a phrase after years of study
to explain why we stay in hopelessness
with men who leave our faces bloody;
why we 'let' the cruel fists of a man
determined to turn our bodies
into a purple storm that began
and ended with fingers that disembody
our self respect, our courage
in that moment, we forget we are somebody.
There is a hierarchy to his chaos
that one learns to simply accept.
There is a beginning to his madness
that one knows will eventually end.
So like those caged animals
they outlawed in circuses,
you let the ringmaster be tyrannical
even as your soul winces.
Years from now, they will ask you
'Why didn't you leave him?'
Because, you will say quietly,
he had convinced me
           I was no longer human.

An Ocean Called Healing

To heal you must first dive into the deepest ocean you will ever find and you will find it locked in that soft, secret thing you call your heart.

When you first swim into its unfathomable depths, you will first find your darknesses – the memories of your trauma that you sank there to forget.

They will try their best to sink you too, to split you with their shark-like teeth, but if you survive the bleeding they put you through, you will reach where you have kept your anger, chained to an anchor at the bottom of this ocean so it doesn't destroy you, so the rage doesn't eat you in seconds the way a piranha does its prey.

When you unchain it from its anchor, embrace it and kiss it goodbye, you finally find yourself wandering in a water cave made of safety, made of understanding till you finally emerge in the alcove of your soul. The light of it shines like sunlight on your face wet with tears. This is where you are safe. This is where you recover. This is how you bathe in the glow of your own healing.

Baptism

I am still waiting
to baptise myself
in the kind of love
that I can confidently
call my own.

I will wash myself
with water
made of self care,
made of kindness
made of joy.

It is the day
I will finally return
to myself.
Learn how to call
my own arms home.

Graveyards and Gardens

There are graveyards
inside you
made of people
that made you ache,
made of memories
that you barely survived
made of trauma
and heartbreak.

These graveyards
need to become
gardens
where you
plant flowers
that blossom,
for you
to let go.

Your Torment Has Meaning

Everything that terrifies you
these monsters
that keeps you up at night
that torment you
that make you feel small
breakable
unable to breathe
like you should not
exist at all,
you defeat them everyday
just by being alive,
this on its own
proves that you are
enough,
and you already have
everything you need
to survive.

The Bones of Trauma

This trauma will turn my bones
to fossil if I allow it to grow till I am old.
If I accept it creeping through my ribcage
the way ivy slowly ages the walls of a home,
looking deceptively pretty
but slowly corrosive to my very soul.
I will open my flower-like mouth
and let it bleed out from between my lips.
I will open my garden-like heart
and pull at every dark weed till it rips.

Homes

I am done making homes
inside broken hearts
trying to fix the roof
that still leaks tears
over another
and fix broken floorboards
that someone else didn't care for.

Instead,
I will go to
my own house shaped heart.
I will lovingly fix
the shambles
others have left of it
I will adore it till no one else
can ever call it haunted again.

And finally
I will open the doors
and welcome myself home.

Forgiveness

Forgive yourself
for everything you broke
when you were trying to survive.

Let the rain
wash away
your regret.

Let your blood cool
from the rage
you feel against yourself.

Let the rivers
under your skin
bring you home.

To heal you must forgive
your heart, your skin, your body
all of their mistakes.

Reminders about Healing

1.

Your heart was made
to break and heal together,
so stop picking at the wounds
and leave it be.

2.

Some loves come with an expiration date,
like all things that are perishable
these kind of loves rot.

3.

Everyone you love is slowly dying
and if you choose not to love them right
they will die without knowing.

4.

You deserve a love that understands
how you fall apart but piece yourself
back together.

5.

It doesn't matter
if it was only once.

6.

All broken things heal.
Yes, even the ones that look like
they are beyond repair.

7.

If he understood how you needed to be loved he would
    still be here.

Toxic People

Stop looking for people who will hold you still, instead look for people who want to help you fly even if it means you fly away from them, even if it means you never see them again.

Stop looking for people who turn your heart into a city when it is your mind that is a country and needs stimulation more than your heart does.

Stop looking for people who only want your beauty and turn away your chaos and darkness.

Stop looking for people who make you believe that they have gone away when you are right beside them.

Stop looking for people who make you feel haunted by your past mistakes.

Start looking for people who treat you like you are everything even when you feel like you are nothing, who help you understand that even powerful nebulas must fall apart to be reborn as exquisite stars.

Reminiscences

There are reminiscences that only return in pieces.
A moment of pleasure disappearing between a flash of
lips and teeth. A second of achievement lost between the
sound of applause and laughter. An entire good day
returning in fragments of sunshine and deep conversations.
If only there was a way to capture these moments whole
in our memories. If only our minds didn't remember
every detail of every tragedy and instead only kept alive
our happiest memories.

Memories

There are memories we share,
and those we do not.
Some remembrances are too soft, too treasured
to be held by the hands of others,
fawned over and passed around,
like a diamond that must be examined,
exclaimed over, and adored.

Some memories are too precious
to share with anyone.
And that is where we keep
our most cherished recollections
of everything
and everyone
that once made us feel so alive.

Love and the Moon

Always let go when you love someone
if they choose not to stay;
because if they love you
they'll always
know home is with you.

I have always understood this
because the moon sings a siren song
to the wolf in me every night.
But I think of the people I have loved,
the ones waiting for me at home.

And I return home always.
Because love's call
has always been
stronger
than the moon's.

Reinvention

Reinvent yourself.
Over and over again.
Plant new wildflowers
into your spirit.
Set a wildfire inside yourself
and then regrow.
Take the wildest thing about you
and nurture it till it blossoms.
Tend to the sea that resides
inside your heart
and listen to its storms
wash you anew.

How else will you let go
of everything
that causes
you such terrible harm.
If you are still
living inside the old you,
the person
who was so damaged
by it all?

I Love You

The words
'I *love you,*'
are sacred
like the flowers
that you have grown
from seed to full bloom.
Stop corrupting
their holy innocence
by using them
as an apology
for the sins
you commit
against the people
who have handed
their heart to you.

Statistics

The statistics say one in four women will encounter the kind of man who has hunt in his eyes, and a hidden big, bad wolf in his smile.

One in four women may be too kind, too soft, too gentle to recognise wolves like him for what they are.

One in four women may think, 'That is not a wolf, that is a simple wickedness, the kind that will thrill my bones.' And this is not to say one in four women are naïve, this is to say that wolves come in all kinds of shapes and sizes. The kind of shapes that can deceive you. The kind of hearts that look like homes but are actually dens made of the corpses of love.

One in four women will be deceived and then broken, and used and turned into someone they are not.

My fear is this: if one in four women can be fooled by men who are not men at all, how many of us have big, bad wolves walking amongst us, waiting for their prey's vulnerability to call.

For Her

Every day
I thank the girl in me
that believed my life
could still be
something magical
even when the darkness
was enough to chew her up,
and spit her out
even when the ledge
was close enough
for her to end it all.

She still chose life.
And I owe it to her
to make something incredible
of myself.

On the days I succeed
I put my hand on my heart
and whisper to her
'This is for you.'

Fairytales exist.
They always have.
We just have to rewrite them
over and over again
till they fit.

Sleeping Beauty

The version of Sleeping Beauty I tell my daughter will be a fairytale about consent before it is a fairytale about true love. In it, I will pause and ask her, 'Do you think it was right for the Prince to kiss a girl who was unconscious, just because he thinks she is pretty?' And I expect her to say 'No. No, it is not.'

In my story, Aurora will not marry the Prince. In my story, Aurora will stand tall, say 'no' to a marriage with a man she barely knows and rule her father's kingdom all on her own.

I will use this story to help her understand, no boy has the right to touch her without her consent just because he thinks she is pretty.

I will teach her to say the word 'No,' before she learns 'Yes.' I will teach her that others may think she is being difficult, but no one's opinion matters as much as her own.

And most important of all, I will teach her never to feel guilty or wear her body as though it is a gift to anyone except herself.

Belle

Belle is fierce in the way lionesses are when they hunt.
She fears nothing and takes on monsters with ease when
it comes to protecting the people she loves. She looks at
someone and sees their inner beauty before she allows
herself to fall in anything close to love. She sacrifices her
freedom, her most treasured possession, for her father.
She stands out from the crowd and reads in a time when
education for women was unheard of. Her kindness and
willingness to give to others is where her true beauty lies.

And yet, in the fairytales we tell our children, we first
introduce her as beautiful rather than fierce, kind,
independent, intelligent, giving, full of light and powerful. Even her name is a testament to outward beauty.

Her name should never have been Belle. Her name should
have been Féroce. Her name should have been Liberté.

Ariel

In this fairytale, Ariel does not look at her childhood, her family, the ocean as though it is something she needs to leave behind for the love of a man. In this fairytale, she chooses her ocean over the Prince because she knows love is something that can happen over and over again, but everything in the ocean that is dying cannot be brought back to life again.

She uses her voice to empower other mermaids to stand against humans destroying their home. She nurses injured sharks and dolphins and fish back to health.

She wears armour, and with her warrior sisters topples poachers' boats leaving them to fight their own way out of the water. She loves her body as it is and does not resent her fish tail and wish for legs or wish to be a land girl because she recognises what she was born in was special. She teams up with the sea witch and encourages her to use her magic to aid in her quest to save the ocean, home to both of them.

And maybe one day, she will fall in love.
And maybe one day, she will find a prince.

Or maybe one day, she will choose never to marry.
Or maybe one day, she will decide to rule instead.

But before she does any of that, for all her hard work for the ocean, she will be remembered.

Snow White

The thing with Snow White is that she isn't so Snow White when the hunter tries to kill her. She grew up in a home with a stepmother who was cruel, which led her to believe that she needed to learn self defense before she sang to the birds or baked apple pie. Because little girls who grow up with the constant threat of a parent who does not love them in their lives learn to listen for foot-steps, watch body language and understand it is they who are responsible for their own little lives.

Imagine, young Snow White in the soldier's training area, wielding a sword, being taught by her father's knights how to overcome any enemy. By the time she is grown, the girl knows her way around a bow and arrow better than she knows around a kitchen and the hunter had no idea what hit him when the princess he thought an easy mark had him on his back, his own sword turned on him in a second.

The seven dwarves didn't give her refuge so she could cook and clean and do their laundry, they gave her refuge because they knew she was the rightful and just heir to the throne, also, they were just decent human beings. And Snow White never bit that apple, because she knew better than to be pressured by strange old ladies she had only just met.

She spent her years in the forest making up an army to reclaim her throne.

Don't ever let them tell you that girls are made for glass boxes and princes and apple pies when girls are made for swords and shields and anything else they damn well want to be.

Cinderella

There is only so much a good person can be verbally insulted and abused before they unleash their inner, sleeping dragon. And this is why Cinderella, locked in her attic, doomed to a life of cleaning, decided enough was enough and decided to take some action.

Cinderella's fairy Godmother wasn't a fairy Godmother at all. She was the best damned lawyer in town, and she took Cinderella's stepsisters and stepmother to the cleaners before they were unceremoniously thrown out of a house that wasn't theirs. At the end of the day, that house was her father's last possession and as its mistress, Cinderella could return it to its former glory and bring back its sunny disposition. She didn't need to worry about balls and glass slippers because she took over her father's business of trading beautifully woven fabric from lands far and wide.

When the Prince did come to her door, he hand delivered her invitation, and Cinderella, who had to leave for a business trip that very evening, told him she had no inclination. She needed no husband at the tender age of nineteen. And she didn't want to become a princess and abandon what she had built, as a royal she would have no time. Because girls who were building empires for themselves did not need kingdoms to shine.

Little Red Riding Hood

Girls who survive trauma wear a certain vulnerability
around them, and some men are wolves, they look for
those girls, their eyes hungry for prey, their tongues filled
with lies to pull girls like this back into the void they have
just escaped from.

Little Red Riding Hood was a survivor too, and once,
when a man had taken a step too far, she had told the story
of what she did to the last thing that tried to devour her.

'I let the wild seep in,' she said, her voice perilously low,
'I let him think he was going to win, but little did he know,
I bare teeth too, sharper than his and a heart that has
survived terrible pain young. When he tried to devour me,
I took the axe from the basket and hacked until he was done.'

If you want to know the secret, if you want to know the
truth, there is nothing more dangerous than a girl who is
aware of the flames inside her, and all the damage she
can do.

Yes. Girls who survive trauma do wear a certain
vulnerability around them, but this kind of vulnerability
is from where their greatest strength stems.

Alice In Wonderland

Alice's rabbit hole began when she entered her father's library and picked up one of the books she was forbidden to read. In it, the words were flavoured with anger and terror and beauty and everything she hadn't tasted yet in her young life. People revolting, war, famine, anger at the aristocracy, compassionate philosophers writing famous ideas and wild theories.

Wonderland emerged when Alice found her love for reading, and even better, acting on what she read. She became a suffragette, fighting for women's rights, and took every scrap of money she was given by her wealthy parents to feed the poor. Alice found a way to use her education for good. She found others like her on the way, and soon she was leading marches and earning the secret name the March Hare, with her suffragette friends who had their own nicknames, like the Mad Hatter for the leader who organised the protests and the White Rabbit for the woman who made sure everyone could safely leave a situation and the Queen of Hearts for the girl who could always charm their way out of police clutches.

She scorned the idea that young ladies of that time should not do what she did. Make change and make waves and create a world more equal for everyone that lives in it.

She was more concerned about making a change and in every little way she could find, she would.

And on the way, she found herself, an incensed, impassioned and extremely capable young woman, all because she let nothing ever stop her from making a change and nothing and no one ever could.

Heroes

We have to heal.
Even from the trauma
that we thought
we would never
heal from.

We have to tend
to our wounds
with water,
and love,
and the moon
and rekindle our fire.

We have to treat
our broken hearts
with kindness,
the kindness
we never received
from anyone else.

Because if we do not
choose ourselves,
if we simply stare
at our pain
and allow it to overcome us
then we lose ourselves forever.

We feed ourselves
so many stories
of princes and saviours
coming to protect us
from our monsters,
from our demons,
that we forget there
is nothing more beautiful,
more fulfilling,
than becoming our own heroes,
than saving ourselves.

Girls of the Wild

They won't tell you fairytales
of how girls can be dangerous and still win.
They will only tell you stories
where girls are sweet and kind
and reject all sin.
I guess to them it's a terrifying thought,
a Red Riding Hood
who knew exactly
what she was doing
when she invited the wild in.

Love yourself loudly, dangerously, everywhere people have been afraid to love you, afraid to ask the way to cherish you, afraid to hold you. Love yourself most in these places, because who can be a better teacher to others in how to love you than you yourself.

Who You Are

You are a gentle, loving person
who has been told
by too many people
that you are difficult to love
and therein lies your torment.

The Epiphany

I did not realise how little
I loved myself
until I understood
that when there
Were four of us in a room
I only counted three.
I finally grasped that in a room
in which there were other people
I always forgot to count me.

Loving What is Broken

It is the way
of the world
to teach us that the things
that others desire
most about you
that you learn
to love most
about yourself.

Your flame hot flesh,
your capacity to give
without taking,
your inability to say no
in the face of love,
your quickness to amend,
your ability to nurture
without nourishment
for yourself.

But have you considered
that it is the parts of you
that are broken
which others
refuse to love
that need your affection
the most?

The Becoming

You became.
When you believed you were nothing.
When everything you loved deserted you.
When you crawled out of the abyss.
When the darkness was so great
it swallowed you whole.
When failure tried to pinch
your soul between its greedy fingers.
When everyone you cared for broke your heart.

This woman that you are today,
You became her by breaking
Over and over and over again.

Allow no one to take that away from you.
You are valuable. You are precious.
Because you built yourself from shards.

You broke to become.

When The Monster Calls

The monster inside your head is smiling as he soaks in the moonlight of your mind. 'You are,' he growls, his languid, dark, body rising as a dark, clawed paw reaches inside your memories, 'a pretty thing on the outside, but who will ever find a way to handle these mangled insides of yours?' His claws gently strum through your memories, as though they are his private collection of music, until he pulls out your greatest nightmare and holds it up, victorious. 'This,' he clucks softly, 'is how you lose everyone.'

The terrible thing he holds is a kerosene sodden, dark laced memoir of trauma and tragedy. A thing that still makes you awaken sweat drenched and trembling in the middle of the night. It is the moment that changed every-thing. The secret you are still mourning, all these years later. And almost every night since it happened, the monster arrives to torment you with it.

Do you know what you must do the next time the fiend calls?

First you must stop calling him a monster at all. For the greatest weapon he and that terrible memory have over you, is your fear of the fall. They depend on you being scared instead of doing what you have to do. He stands between you and your journey into healing. So you must face him bravely, you must survive the breaking. The monster is simply your beautiful, broken mind, trying to convince you to let go. And when you finally face him, take the memory from his hands, understand that it was not your fault. This is how you will deal with it when chaos ever calls.

Survival

Everyone you love
is capable of doing
great and terrible things
things you never
thought they could do
when they are clawing,
panicking,
breaking
to survive.
Remember this
when you watch them
at their very worst moments.
And forgive them
their survival too.

Journey

Compare your journey to no one else.
You are countries and stories already.
You are a million different words,
a million different ways.
You are forests and forest fires alike
A ship and the sea together.

The only person
you must compare
yourself with
is yourself.

Your journey
is your most powerful story.

Boys will be Boys

I want to ask everyone who says 'Boys will be boys' how often they say 'Girls will be girls.'

You see, the last time I heard these words from a woman about her son when she had heard about him pulling a little girl's hair in the playground I asked if she would say the same about girls, her smile fell from her face as she said 'It is different for girls.' And my mouth filled with acid, contempt, all the words I could not say.

I want to say, 'It is different for girls, because we have made it so. We have created a world where our daughters are held responsible for not just their own actions, but for the actions of men. We make our daughters suffer for how our sons treat them. Is it not burden enough to grow up in a world that is already more unkind to women than it is to men? I refuse to excuse my sons for behavior I would not tolerate from my daughters. I refuse to burden my daughters with the consequences of men's actions against them.' But instead, I bit my tongue and stayed silent, as thousands before me have.

A month later, I was told that the little girl had punched the boy in the eye for pulling her hair one time too many. His parents were furious and demanded action. She was taken to the principal's office and forced to apologise to him, then disciplined appropriately. And not once was anyone ready to excuse her behavior as 'Girls will be girls.'

And I still wonder, 10 years later, if the lesson she learned for standing up for herself was that no one comes running to protect little girls when it is little boys they are standing up against.

Three Sentences

'I believe you.'
'You did nothing wrong.'
'This was not your fault.'

Three sentences that can turn a victim into a survivor.
Three sentences that are not used nearly enough.

Hostage

'I love you,'
they weep, their hands around your throat.
'I love you,'
they say, as they betray you again
'I love you,'
they whisper as they touch the orchid-like bruises
they have left across your skin.
'I love you,'
they murmur as they force their hands
where they do not belong

How cruel it is
to be held hostage
by a love
that you genuinely believe
will one day be good
when it will always
be ruthless with your soul.

Silence

The tragedy is people see you as a victim
and they keep seeing you as a victim
because you talk about the thing that hurt you.
Because you talk about your trauma
Because you discuss the thing that tore you apart.

They do not understand that talking about it
Being brave enough to face it
understanding it
and allowing others
to see all of your vulnerability
is courage at its rawest.

You are a survivor
because you are not silent
Do not allow others
to define your survival
Because they lack the patience
The understanding
The courage to hear it.

There is nothing convenient
about freedom.
It is born from battle cries
and war, and blood,
and death
and people living for it
and dying for it
without ever getting it.

Never let anyone
tell you that it was easy
for you to have the fire,
the storms, the oceans
of strength
to speak your mind
that you have today.

The Truth about Art

People don't look at art because it's perfect. People look at art because it's extraordinary, strange, different, captivating, odd, unusual, they look at it because it stands out. Some artwork is so entrancing, people spend hours looking at it and in awe of its strangeness. Sometimes entire rooms are dedicated to one masterpiece so it is given its proper glory. Perfection is boring. It is stereotypical. It blends together and it's easily forgotten.

What I'm trying to say is,
You can strive to be perfect.
Or you can strive to be art.

Fire

Remember what you must do
when they undervalue you,
when they think
your softness is your weakness,
when they treat your kindness
like it is their advantage.

You awaken
every dragon,
every wolf,
every monster
that sleeps inside you
and you remind them
what hell looks like
when it wears the skin
of a gentle human.

Wild

I looked at everything wild
the birds in the trees,
the lions in their paradise,
the foxes and their prey
and thought:

'Have you ever had to try
to make someone love you?'
and my answer came to me
like the wind whispering
it from the wild to my ears.

Never.
Never.
Never.

Weathered

The cliffs may seem magnificent.
But the truth is the cliffs are only there because the sea
has whittled them down over time, the water weathering
and wearing against the rock. From this, I learned that no
matter how large my problems are, or how big they seem,
if I work on them every single day eventually they too will
be worn as can be.

Why She Stayed

And before
you ask her
why she stayed,
look at the way
a caged bird
sometimes
refuses to leave,
even when
its cage door
is wide open.
Even when
you call it
softly.
Even when you
try to take it
out of its prison
to set it free.

And perhaps then
you will understand.

Her Skin

Did you really think
that your hands on her skin
would diminish her worth?

Did you imagine that your manhood
was more powerful
than her womanhood?

She will grow,
her skin shed from the woman you had
to the woman she has become.

She will rise,
above your petty labels of slut and whore
to the woman who stands for none of it.

She will ascend,
like a battle cry
from a war you thought you had won.

She will intensify,
the way the ocean does
to take entire ships in her storm.

And when she has risen,
she will unleash on you how strong,
how truly powerful is her whole worth.

You are Everything

Remember that everything that men use is named for a woman. Every car, every plane, every ship, every bomb, every weapon, we refer to them as 'her' and 'she'. Because deep down, they know that without 'she' and 'her', our very existence is limited. Without 'she' and 'her', the human race cannot survive. So wear your existence with the command, with the dominance it was born into. And never allow the world to convince you that you are anything less than the life giver that you are. You are power. You are everything. You are the architect of your own beautiful, wild chaos, your own destiny, woman. And no one can ever take that from you unless you let them.

Desecration

Every time a man takes
from a woman's body
without her permission,
he is disrespecting the womb
from which he was born,
he is defiling the place
that protected him
when he was
at his most defenceless,
he is desecrating the temple
where he began his journey.

Pity these men,
then show them
what destruction looks like
when it wears the body
of a woman
who has been wronged.

Mythology

Woman,

Remember you are Pandora.
You hold the key to a box
full of terror and hope in your hands
and only you can destroy the world
or start it anew.

Remember you are Persephone.
Emerging from the darkness
when all hope was lost
embracing even hell
in all its fearsome terror.

Remember you are Hera.
The queen that brought
Gods and demi Gods
to their knees in terror
of her supreme power.

You are a myth born to the wrong age. You are the kind of book
that has magical stories trapped in every single page.

Helen

Pretty girls have it easy, her mother always said to her whilst brushing her hair. And for a while, Helen was happy with knowing she was so pretty that she would always get her way.

Until she grew old enough to understand that pretty wasn't easy. Pretty meant she could be used. Pretty meant that men would fight not over her, but over her beauty. Pretty meant that she was reduced to just a thing, property to be sold to the highest bidder. When the men came to ask for her hand, whether she was ready or not, she had to choose her husband, not a lover.

But Helen had a secret, a secret none of the men who claimed to love her would ever know. The blood that ran in her veins was not human, it was ichor. She was the daughter of the most powerful God, her half brothers Apollo, Achilles, and power, power was so much more important than beauty ever could be.

And Paris was sweet, and innocent in the way none of the men she had been with. But she didn't run for him. She would never run for anyone, other than herself. Helen had never belonged to anyone the way she had belonged to herself. And her face may have launched a thousand ships, but that is what you get when a girl who learned that she had a dormant Goddess inside her finally began to awaken and become fire itself.

Aphrodite

Her mother named her Aphrodite, because in her eyes,
there was nothing and no one she could ever love so well.
And Aphrodite is beautiful, but she is beautiful in the way
of the sea. The kind of beauty magazines can't handle, but
poets and storytellers can wile away hours writing about,
and to which musicians compose symphonies.

Every morning she looks into the mirror and smiles,
admiring the twinkle in her dark eyes, the sheer beauty
in her skin that is the colour of a night storm, and her
hair the glistening colour of the night sky. Her waist and
legs are thick, her figure fuller than any girl she has ever
seen in any magazine, but she loves her body because she
knows that they are wrong and she is right.

She walks with confidence, almost floating above the
people who do not understand her, who do not treasure
her kind of beauty. But Aphrodite has always known she
is special despite their wagging tongues, their inconse-
quential gossip designed to be cruel. She knows because
the night sky once kissed the ocean and that was the day
she was born. She knows because her mother always told
her, she could be anything she wants because her beauty is
boundless, her essence incredible . . .

And never once, no matter what others say, has she
ever doubted her own beauty,
her own worth.

Artemis

Girls like Artemis are made of volcanoes and earthquakes, everything that scares people and the world can't handle. They were made for beautiful things, for bigger things. So when people try to put them in a box, try to turn them into something they can understand, girls like Artemis simply fight harder.

You see, no matter how much you tell a girl like Artemis to be a lady, to stop her eternal hunt, to understand that the moon is not her true lover, that the way she dresses is not appropriate, she will do exactly how she pleases. Nothing ties her down to the kind of earth you have come from. Nothing makes her want to be less adventurous or give up her eternal search for something to quench her wanderlust.

She is different and she wears her individuality on her worn jacket, the one her mother has tried to throw away countless times but always comes back, her eyes always hunting for something more beautiful than the moment before her right now. She has been hurt before, but always, always has found her way back from the pain. You see, her heart was born a wolf. If anyone has tried to break it with their callousness, it has always gone for their throat.

Athena

Fall in love with a girl who spends her time lost in stories.
Let her beguile you with versions you never knew about
history, about the world, the strangest things that can
ever be told. Allow her to bring you truths that you never
thought would be spoken, the kind of depth and wisdom
that you thought the world had long since broken. See in
her eyes the stories that once moved you as a child.

Fall in love with a girl who would rather resolve the
mysteries of the universe. Let her take you through time in
a way you never imagined possible. Watch her lead you all
the way across the cosmos with simple words and phrases
that you never imagined could have such an effect on you.
Science seems to bend to her will, but if you say this to her,
she will shake her head and deny it with a smile.

Fall in love with a girl who values wisdom above all else.
Let her become Athena, the Goddess of Wisdom before
your eyes and see the world in a way you never thought
possible. Let her make you spin in ways you never
thought could happen. In the end of it all, she will
become something different, something special.
Something that no one else will ever be able to fully
replace in your heart.

Fall in love with a girl who has a softness and an intelligence to her. The kind of girl who is always hidden away in libraries, hungry for knowledge, who grows excited over facts.

Yes. Fall in love with a girl like that.

Persephone

When people talk of Persephone, they always turn her into a victim. She was a wood nymph that was so innocent that Hades stole her away from her mother and brought her to a prison.

What if the real story was something completely different? What if it was Persephone in control and not Hades at all? What if she was bored of the flowers, discontent with her situation and wanted to make more of her life than the grass and the trees could offer her?

What if she asked Hades to take her away? And the God of the Underworld hesitated, but her sheer ambition, her fire just swept him away?

On earth, she was just the daughter of a Goddess, the quiet, pretty wood nymph who played in a forest.

But in the underworld, she is given a throne made of fire, a crown made of thorns and the fear and exaltation of the dead as they watch her in awe.

Persephone is the very definition of spirit and determination. She didn't just wait for someone to come and rescue her from her discontent and strife, instead she took matters into her own hands and empowered her own future, her own life.

Hera

In this story, Zeus is every bad guy we ever fell in love with, coming home late at night or sometimes not at all, stinking of alcohol and other women, promising Hera every time she meets him in the morning, sleeping on the couch that one day, one day he's going to change and he's going to become a better person but that day isn't today.

And Hera is the kind of woman who has the resilience and belief that one day he will change. Even when he screams at her. Even when he loses his mind at her, even when he tells her she is unlovable. And she believes in him all the way until one day, she sees him stagger home and he has forgotten once again that it is her birthday.

She locks the door and just listens to him hammer for hours. Clenching her teeth, because it would be so easy to just let him back into her life. She takes her heart and locks it away. Because she knows it's too fragile to make any decisions right now. Her courage is made of pain and heartache and trauma but it is still courage in every way it can be.

At nights, she sleeps in a bed made of her own worst fears of not having him there and slowly, she grows accustomed to sleeping by herself. She grows accustomed to her own company. She doesn't answer his calls. She doesn't respond when he rings the doorbell. She takes her life and starts turning it into something beautiful without him. She learns how to love herself in the most intricate of ways. She goes out and spends times with her friends when she is lonely. She learns to love her alone. And often when she finds herself missing him, missing the good moments with him, she whispers to herself 'The absence of you has taught me how to love myself. So thank you, my darling, my dearest.'

Demeter

To understand Demeter's heartache,
Think of every mother who broke her own heart
Time and time again to give her children a better future.

The mothers who walked away
from abusive spouses,
the mothers who faced danger
for their children
the mothers who broke their backs
just to give their children a better future,
the mothers who chose their children's comfort
over their own every time.

And all this at the same time as nurturing us
from root to sapling to trees to forest.

There is no greater love.
There never will be.

You need not fear the wolves you hide in your soul. They were made not to hurt you, but to protect you against this world.

Too Much

There is a sky inside you
and it is made of flames
and it is made of rain.
But you refuse to release it
because someone you loved
once told you that you are too much
to handle when you unleash
all of your beauty,
your passion,
your vulnerability.
You are too much
when you are raw.

So instead, you hide it.
You hold in the storms
you slowly let the fire die.
All because you think
how no one can handle
your truth, your courage,
your pain.

Daughters

When you see your daughter falling into that trap the mirror has been creating for you and every woman before you: 'Your nose is too long, look at that acne, you have strange eyes,' a thousand flaws on one small form, pull her aside and remind her that mirrors aren't a true reflection of the person you are on the inside.

Teach her that her body is her most beautiful, powerful gift. The way it heals her. The way it sacrifices for her. The way it aches. Every single one of its flaws aren't flaws at all, they are there for a reason. Teach her about the ocean and how she protects the many lives within her. Teach her how her body is like the ocean, protecting the many parts of her that are so alive.

And eventually she will understand that everything about her is magic, and her body will breathe a sigh of relief and love her for it.

Courage

The way you love
passionate and all encompassing
is not something you should be ashamed of.
If they could not handle your passion
if they were scared by it
if they now make you feel guilty
for loving them too much
don't you dare allow them
to make you doubt the courage
you carry like the sea in your soul.

You are not too emotional or weak.
Your courage is determined
by the room in your heart
to love over and over again,
despite having it broken
by so many who were unworthy of you.

Son

I hope when your son cries
you do not tell him he's a girl
because you will always remember
his mother's bravery
when she gave birth to him.

Or when he chooses a pink t-shirt
instead of a blue one
you leave his choices alone.

Or when he prefers art
to football and sports,
you applaud him.

Or when he expresses emotions
you encourage him
to express them more often.

Or when he chooses a man
instead of a woman to marry
you remember he is still your son.
And nothing will ever change
the love you have for him.

Self Care

Sometimes the people you love the most are the ones that will cause you the most pain. And you will forgive them and continue to have them in your life. This does not make your pain invalid. This does not mean you should allow them to ignore it. This does not mean they are allowed to hurt you again. Continuing to trust someone who was the reason behind your hurt is no reason to allow them to hurt you the same way again. No matter how much they apologise and say they will change. No matter how much they try to guilt you and place blame. No matter how often they call you selfish for not forgiving them yet again. This is the meaning of self care. This is the meaning of self preservation. And you are never wrong to practice it.

Let Go

What holds you back is not your ability to let go. It is your ability to hold on and keep hoping on things that have not loved you enough to give so many chances to. One day, you will encounter a sea of tears and realise it is your own. And it will both break and mend your heart.

Only then will you move on.

Secret Language

We have always felt so unsafe in this world
Like soldiers, always on the alert
A secret language between us women
are you safe?

Have you reached home?
Did anyone follow you?
Because we have come to understand
that no one is going to protect us but each other.

And this bond of sisterhood is so sacred
I hope it one day destroys
the idea that women are competition
for each other.

Instead enforces
how much
we belong in
our fierceness for each other.

Fossilised Love

Sometimes I go digging
for memories of you
inside my own chest,
the way an archaeologist
does for fossils.
You are more precious
to me in memory,
less dangerous,
the same way
a carnivorous dinosaur is
in a museum.

And I wonder
how many of us are still
carrying our love
as fossils in our hearts?

Hunted

How do little girls with such happiness in their footsteps grow up to become hunted women? Where do they begin to start wearing that look of prey in their eyes? Where does that beautiful sparkle go? How does such innocence that comes from the sea and the stars turn into something that is so terrified of its own shadow?

And what do you do to bring it all back again? How do you turn hunted women into happy, carefree little girls again.

Primitive

The way we project love on our televisions, on cinema screens, at parties, the long walks on the beach, walks in the rain, none of this is real. People talk of love like it is patient and it is kind. Love is also dark. It is ferocious and angry and destructive. If you do not believe me: look at how a mother wolf protects her young. Look at how all the wild protects each other. And then ask yourself; do you really know what love is?

Precipice of Loss

Listen if you are there at the precipice of losing yourself, I will give you the advice I wish I could have given myself when I was thirteen years old, still on the training wheels of life, where loss and grief had not decided to make a ghost out of me, yet I could not understand the sadness that was trying to devour me from within. There, alone, sitting on the floor of my bedroom, making a list of people who would be happier if I was gone, it never occurred to me that the only person I really need to live for is myself. There I was, wishing, praying for love in the arms of everyone else, and it never hit me for even a second, here, just take those two arms you already have and wrap them around yourself.

If I could see her again, I would say as I say to you now: look, look at all of the things you can accomplish all on your own. You will rise, simply because you believe in yourself, you need no one else to believe in you. You will go through devastation and draw your own body out of the wreckage, time and time again. You will rescue yourself from drowning because you taught yourself how to swim out of grief. Other people do not matter. No one on that list is coming to save you, the person who will save you, time and time again, already exists inside you. Whisper her an incantation, awaken her the way one awakes a sleeping dragon. You may have been given wars in this life, but in you there lies an army, you just have to know their battle cry. There is no justice in the world. You have to make your own, because believe me, the cosmos that gifted you the chaos, also created you with care.

Reset

Sometimes I wonder if the Gods created
our bodies to reset because they knew the destruction that
was going to be hailed on them.

As if they knew we would not know better
in how to look after our bodies
and heal minds at the same time ourselves.

For your healing wasn't just a path of tears.
For every part of you that came together was stitched
together with heartache.

Surviving

We live in a world
that would rather ask women
why did you stay
with someone who hit you,
than ask why the man
she had trusted with her love
had betrayed her,
had the audacity to think
he had any right to hit her.
We laud abusive men,
celebrate their success
despite knowing about
the accusations against them,
say that the women
who accuse them are liars,
and even if proved right,
say that she is trying
to destroy him.
That she must have
provoked him.

And therein,
I think,
lies the problem.

We blame women
for the very violence that
destroys their lives.

Therapy

The therapist used words like 'trauma' and 'abuse' like
they were so commonplace. I think that is what scares me
most. That the way they held my soul down and took from
me in every way possible was nothing new.

That my bloodied and broken spirit was one of many that
had walked into this office before. That she had heard this
story so often, she had turned clinical from empathetic.

And then the fear turned to anger. How many of us are
out there? How many of us have been destroyed this way?
How many of us have been left on the precipice of death
and no one cared? How many? How many?

And when were these bloodied spirits they had ripped
apart going to finally heal? And I knew then in asking
myself the question there was an answer. It is when a
sheep like myself rejects her sheepskin for that of a wolf.
It is when a sheep like myself chooses to become a
warrior.

I hope every single one of us that ache become stronger
every day. That we all channel our inner wolves and turn
into warriors in every way.

They may have taken us down individually, but they cannot destroy an army made of us all.

Small Magic

On the days my sickness talks to me,
I remember small magic.
I remember the way the pretty ivy
outside my window entwines
with white wood.
I remember the way the rain
softly taps against my window
to help me fall asleep.
I remember the way the universe
loved me so much, that inside my body's cell,
it placed little universes that are its mirror image.
I remember the way I am loved
by the few people
I know will never leave.
And I allow the small magic
to sing so loud and so happy in my ears
that my sickness forgets how to speak.

Temporary

Like the leaves of the trees
that shed and leave with the wind
never remembering how to return
never coming back again
so shall you be temporary to people
who have loved you deeply too.
Remember this when you are cursing others
for leaving and wishing them back to you.

Pandora's Box

There are days I feel
my womanhood is a burden.

Days when I must be
conscious of what I wear
because I do not wish
to get unwanted attention.

Days my breasts and my legs
don't feel like they belong to me.

Days I cannot look men in the eye
because I do not want them to get
the wrong idea about me.

It's because we are taught
from an early age
that we hold within our bodies
Pandora's box.

Something so dangerous
it does not just affect us,
it affects everyone we love,
and everything we care for.

And we must guard it with strength,
with determination,
hiding ourselves from becoming
an object of lust and sexual appetite.

Still I cannot help but wonder
as often as I did as a child.
Why do we shame Pandora for opening the box,
when she simply did it out of curiosity?

Shouldn't we rather blame the person
who created a box
of such terrible power
as we should blame society
for making rules for our bodies
that we never agreed to,
nor wanted to be our philosophy?

Temple

Her body is not your home
it is a temple
and you are a pilgrim
it is kindly giving shelter to.
And pilgrims know better
than to destroy the holy thing
that is providing them with shelter
away from their home.

Questions to Ask Yourself

When was the last time
someone was kind to you
without wanting anything
from you?

When was the last time
someone was gentle with your soul
without asking for something
in return?

Value

I only learned
the value,
the weight,
the density
of my soul
when people tried
to devalue,
undermine
and soil it
with terrible intentions
with their damning touch.

Pieces

I understand
your need to nurture
and to give yourself away in pieces.

But darling,
some people will take from you
and give nothing back in return.

You feel empty souled and heavy hearted,
it is because you have been robbed
of your kindness.

Protect that kind, giving heart,
give to those who appreciate
your magnificent soul.

Time

What I have spent
in mourning
is the price
I have paid
for my healing.

Belonging

You have belonged
better in your own arms
than in anyone else's.

Remember you are
the softest love
you will ever have.

Haunted

We are all preoccupied,
haunted by the people
we should be.
By the ghosts of everything
we promised ourselves
as children we would be,
until we faced life with all its cruelty
and it turned us into graveyards
of our dreams, our choices,
of what should have been our history.

Nurture

Yesterday
I spent the morning
tending to my wounds
with the sun's rays
and brushing through my scars
with sweet, honey like words.
I spent the afternoon
washing my sins away
with warm salt water.
I spent the evening
in the moonlight
soothing my mind
under its calm.

Later,
my mother asked me
what I did that day,
I told her,
'I healed.
For my soul,
like flowers
needs tending too.'

Blossom

Recognise the danger
of loving someone
who does not let
the seeds of your emotions
blossom
whether in tears or flowers.
If they cannot empathise,
they should not be
a part of your life.

My Monsters

I had hoped one day to find someone
who loves my monsters,
the wolves that I feed,
the demons I sing to sleep
the tiger that is my caged heart
the parts of me I do not talk about
I prayed and wished and yearned
until I realised that I had already found her
within me.

Never Forget

Woman,

Forget what anyone tells you.
Your flaws are beautiful.
Sit down with them
and admire them.

You are permitted to be cruel sometimes.
And you are allowed to fall apart,
and feel every emotion
they tell you not to feel.

People tell you to be virtuous,
and ladylike and pretty
and everything you aren't
and were never going to be.

People forget that women too
sometimes bare teeth.
We too feel the need to be hard
and lustful and angry and taste blood.

Just because we are soft
doesn't mean there aren't flames
within us that rise
a thousand miles above.

Fuel

The fuel that runs this spirit, this soul,
is not easy to understand.
It is made of fire
And it is made of water.
It is made of the kind of darkness
that will swallow entire stars.
But it is also made
of the cold sea waves
that soothe.

It is wild too,
as wild as the birds
and wolves
that live in the forest.
And the way it flies
when we experience true happiness,
true freedom
it is made of the wind too.

We try to classify ourselves
into words,
into labels,
but how to define
something as eternal,
as huge as your soul
when it is an entire universe
in and of itself?

Three Versions of You

There are three versions of you.
The one that smiles
and laughs with others,
the one that hides
and cries alone,
and the one that has the ability
to achieve greatness.
These are like three roots
that emerge from a sapling,
you must find a way to grow
into a single, enlightened being
like a wise old oak,
and you will bear the fruit
of every happiness that eludes you.

Earth

When you are in pain
remind yourself
of the earth and
how she must have felt
when she was born.
Every single one of
her oceans
her rivers
her forests
and her sky
must have
caused her agony
in creation.
And from her,
you will learn this:
growth is a thing
of beauty
and of pain,
without heartache
there are no lessons
to gain.

Planets and Stars

And if they berate you
and push you down
and break you
and tell you over and over again
how you are not enough,
remember how Pluto
had once been dissolved
to being nothingness,
and is fighting its way back
into being a planet again.

You are made of planets
and stars and seas and oceans.
And no one can tell them
what they can and cannot be.

Just like no one can tell you
what you can and cannot be.

Bedtime Stories

When your daughter asks you to tell her bedtime stories,
the kind that you grew up with, I hope you tell her
better versions.

I hope you tell her bedtime stories where the princess isn't
a princess but a knight and she's going to war with dragons
all by herself. I hope you tell her stories where the princess
rescues her father's kingdom from impending doom.
I hope you tell her stories where girls save themselves
from anything. And no towers and monsters and dragons
and kings can ever stop them from doing what they want
to do.

Acknowledgements

With deepest gratitude to:

My parents for letting me grow at my own pace and in my own time, the way I need.

My grandparents for always telling me the best stories and truths.

My brother for being so supportive and strong when I needed him.

Emma, for discovering my work, being the absolute best editor anyone could wish for and keeping me inspired always.

Leanne, Zabiba and Cait for being the dream team of wonder women every author should be blessed with.

Steve, for being there for me when I had broken and thought would never recover.

Ivan and Tom for being such incredible humans in a world where that is becoming difficult.

Clare, for being my sister and my human when I needed one the most.

Bianca and Chris, for believing in the crazy universes and theories I can only share with them.

Tree and Jo for being the once-in-a-lifetime friends that they are and who never fail to bring joy and creative life wherever they go.

And to you, who has never stopped believing in good, and watching the night sky, no matter what life has thrown at you. Thank you for believing always. I hope you find what you are looking for.

About the Author

Nikita Gill is a British-Indian writer and poet living in the south of England. With a huge online following, her words have entranced hearts and minds all over the world.

Follow her work online:
Instagram: @nikita_gill
Tumblr: meanwhilepoetry.tumblr.com
Facebook: f/nikitagillwrites
Twitter: @nktgill